The

Best of
Both Worlds
Theory

23
Keys To
Motivation
Self-Improvement
&
Living A Better Life!

Eric J. Safranek

THE BEST OF BOTH WORLDS THEORY™
Eric J. Safranek

AvanVive Publishing™
Orlando, Florida USA
www.AvanVive.com

AvanVive, AvanVive Publishing, and all other AvanVive
subsidiaries are Trademarked and exclusive property of
Eric J. Safranek.

*A portion of all proceeds from this book will be donated to
charitable causes all around the world!*

First Print Edition

ISBN-13: 978-1508663324
ISBN-10: 1508663327

DISCLAIMER

This book is solely for entertainment and informational purposes. The concepts, suggestions and medical advice throughout this book as well as the supporting audio, video, and website materials, including but not limited to Avanvive.com, solely express the opinions and beliefs of the author.

I am NOT a Medical Doctor.
I do not claim to be a Medical Doctor.

This book and it's supporting materials are simply a collection of my beliefs, based upon my years of reading, research, real world experiences and conclusions. I recommend that you do your own research and consult your personal physician before altering or starting any new exercise regimen or diet.

Please...question what I say, what your Doctor says and whatever you may see on TV! If something does not agree with your beliefs or gut instincts, then I suggest that you follow your intuition and seek out better advice. The Author, Publisher and AvanVive expressly disclaim responsibility from any adverse effects you may encounter from following any suggestions or information within this book.

What worked for me, may not work for you. At the end of the day, you are the one who is responsible for all the decisions and actions that you choose to pursue.
Please use common sense and stay safe.

Good Luck and Good Health!

AvanVive Publishing™

DEDICATION

*This book is dedicated to
all the great women
that have impacted my life
for the better.*

*From the women that have taught me
the numerous lessons over the years
to the ones that still guide me today!*

My Mother Ruth
My Gramma Anne
My Aunt Phyllis
My Friend J-Lo
My Sister Samantha
Mi Mama Lilliam
My Wife Paula

*I hope that the next generation of
mothers, fathers and leaders
will be guided by the same great
Morals and Values
that all these women
shared in common
and instilled upon me.*

In Memory of

Thomas J. Roozen

April 2, 1941 – November 22, 2014

CONTENTS

Message From The Author

SECTION I
INTRODUCTION

SECTION II
OPTIMIZE YOUR HEALTH

SECTION III
CULTIVATE YOUR MIND

SECTION IV
SATISFY YOUR SOUL

SECTION V
CONCLUSION

SECTION VI
BONUS CHAPTER

The
Best of Both Worlds
Theory

MESSAGE FROM THE AUTHOR

I am sorry...

I want to apologize to my readers that purchased this book with the expectations of a traditional book with predictable styles and a properly formatted work of literature. I have taken the liberty of bucking traditional and conventional layouts for one of a more poetic and artistic approach in order to more creatively share my knowledge and observations with the World. This way, I hope to present my message to the reader by getting right to the point instead of burying it amongst pages of fluff. I stick to the philosophy of, "Don't say in ten words what you can say in five."

My voice is that of a casual conversation between me and my reader – not of a proper literary work that abides by all the restrictive rules.

This book is a continuation and expansion upon ideas and concepts which I first laid out in my original book, *"Happy, Healthy, Wealthy & Wise."* I have learned over the years that several different approaches may be necessary in order to get the same message across to a variety of people.

Where my original book did an excellent job of delivering the overall message within a simple short story, this book excels in delivering more insights into the specific lessons and actual philosophy that the first book was originally based upon.

I would highly suggest reading this book with a highlighter to emphasize the lessons that best relate to you **Right Now**. Over the years, as you look back upon and reread this book, I truly believe that more lessons will become relatable to you as new events transpire throughout your lifetime.

Enjoy!

SECTION I

INTRODUCTION

PREFACE

IT WAS A PLEASANT SUMMER DAY back in July of 1985 when we were returning back to our house in Naperville, Illinois. My sister and I had just spent the night at my Aunt and Uncle's house in St. Charles to hang out and play with our cousin Amy for the weekend.

While growing up, we were inseparable. We were the "Three Amigos!" My sister Samantha was ten and both my cousin Amy and I were twelve. We believed that we would be spending one more night at their house, but my Aunt insisted instead that we head back first thing this morning. I had my suspicions why, but the truth was far worse.....

As we arrived back home to our house in the rural Chicago suburb of Naperville, we were greeted by our dogs, Misty and Box.....Yes, Box! When I was just four years old, my father allowed me to name the one brown puppy from Misty's litter of black and white puppies. I wasn't too creative at that age and noticed that we kept the entire litter of puppies in a big brown box right after they were born, hence the name... Box!

After maneuvering our way through the dogs, the first person I saw was my Uncle Tom standing behind our bar in the living room. That was kinda weird, I thought to myself, what was he doing over here? I was wondering where he had disappeared off to this morning.

Finally we were greeted with a huge hug and kiss from our father. After giving his sister a quick hug, my father said that he had to speak with my sister and I privately upstairs.

I nervously grabbed a few Nutter Butter cookies from the kitchen on the way upstairs to his bedroom as I had this
horrible . . . sinking – – – feeling . . .

It was there that he sat us down and explained to us that our mother had just passed away earlier that morning. After years of battling breast cancer, she finally succumbed to the disease. My mother was only thirty-nine years old and my now widowed father was thirty-eight.

So there we were, in my parent's bedroom, just the three of us balling our eyes out and me with two crushed Nutter Butter cookies in my right hand attempting to digest the worst news of my life. Without a final, "I Love You" or a single, "Goodbye" she was gone.

Even though others may have known, I was oblivious to the possibility that she may actually die. To say that her death caught me off guard would be an understatement. It hit me hard. Everything changed in an instant, right at that very moment. This one event would forever alter the direction and focus of my life.

I have personally struggled with depression, fear and low self-esteem issues for years. It is still something that my sister, (who was only ten years old at the time of my mother's passing) is still trying to deal with today, some thirty years later. Over the years I started jotting down some notes and thoughts. I also looked to music for direction and escape. As my musical horizons expanded, I came across the album "5150" by one of my favorite bands, Van Halen. One song in particular peaked my interest...

*"You don't have
To die and go to Heaven,
Or wait around
To be born again,
Just tune in to what this place has got to offer,
'Cause we may never be here again,
I want the Best of Both Worlds...
Heaven right here on Earth"*

–Best of Both Worlds by Van Halen

And with that I started writing down more ideas of how I could, "tune in to what this place has got to offer" and discover my own, "Heaven right here on Earth!" From that point on, I have referred to this philosophy under construction as, "The Best of Both Worlds Theory."

I continued to write throughout the years, never truly aspiring to be an author, but mostly just to sort through my thoughts and to put on paper the person that I had hoped to become... a person that my mother would be proud of. I realized early on that she would be happiest if I were just simply to become..... myself.

It took me some fifteen years before I finally came to terms with my mother's death and was able to move on. This all happened within a single "A-ha!" moment of realization as I was backpacking throughout Australia.

I took this journey to Australia by myself, simply armed with my backpack, a day pack, a round-trip ticket, my Lonely Planet travel guide and a place to stay in Sydney for the first two nights! I played the entire three month stint down there by ear.

I started out by taking a train down to Melbourne for a couple weeks, then bought a Northbound bus pass with unlimited stops to Cairns.

This day of realization came to me as I was staying at a youth hostel in Queensland, Australia. It was a cool and hip party hostel with a little tiki bar in the central courtyard. They hosted nightly barbecues and played movies on a large outdoor screen. It was a very social and fun atmosphere, but unfortunately, I was feeling neither fun nor social that evening. I picked up a bottle of vodka in town and kept to myself despite invitations from others. I went on to polish off most of the bottle that night, which was a common way for me to kill the pain inside, numb the brain and expand my thinking. I reached for my journal and started to write.

As I was writing, my message became more and more Positive. It was at that very moment that I realized what Freedom I had gained right down there in Australia.

Out of the blue, I suddenly remembered a quote from Tony Robbins where he defined what it meant to him to be truly free. He said that freedom to him, was the ability to go, "Wherever I want, whenever I want, with whomever I want, for as long as I want." And that's when it hit me...

I AM FREE! I was living a life that I had previously believed was reserved solely for Millionaires and Billionaires!

I was doing whatever I wanted, with whomever I wanted for as long as I wanted! Here I was taking three months off from work to travel throughout Australia! If I liked a city I stayed, if I didn't, I moved on to the next one. If I made some friends, I would hang out with them, if I got bored, I would simply continue my journey.

I finally came to the realization that this great freedom which I had achieved was all a result of the path that I had chosen... the path that had materialized within the aftermath of my mother's death. I had a choice of many paths to pursue; a path of righteousness, a path of destruction, or one comprised of the multitude of other options available in-between.

The trail I blazed was of my own and all of the supposed mistakes or failures were simply lessons and mile markers along the way. My mother's death forever changed the overall direction of my life and brought me to where I am today, which is exactly where I needed to be!

I thought to myself for just a moment, what if she didn't die? Let's say that I had gone on to live the perfect stereotypical American Dream: go to college, get a job, start a career, get married, have 2.5 kids, a dog and a beautiful house with a white picket fence... only to have a mid-life crisis and wonder why I had never traveled the world or gone to Australia.

I might start to blame the rat race or the wife and the kids for holding me back or something along those lines, but at that very moment, I was right where I needed to be! I was doing exactly what I had always hoped to do.

I was experiencing a Freedom like never before while pursuing my Passion and doing what I loved... Traveling!

My perspective on life has been ever Evolving and more and more Positive ever since that moment of realization! I have continued to travel and develop this philosophy. This path that I have chosen is not an easy one – actually quite the contrary. But I truly believe that these difficulties provide me with the lessons that I needed to master in order to comprehensively form my beliefs.

The book that you hold in your hands right now is a result of that very philosophy that I have been formulating over the past two and a half decades.

I refer to this as a "Philosophy Under Construction" as I constantly aim to expand to, improve upon and perfect these lessons throughout my lifetime.

**The Best of Both Worlds Theory
shall always remain a Theory
until you personally accept
the general premise
of the philosophy**

It has taken me well over twenty-five years to come full circle. I have finally unearthed my own Heaven right here on Earth and it lies in discovering my Purpose and my Passion as well as the Path that I was destined to follow! My Path is one of Self-Improvement. My Passion is to Travel the World. My Purpose is to help others by sharing with them what I learn along the way.

This book is simply a collection of insights, advice, wisdom, lessons, quotes and affirmations that I have both written and collected over the years. These "Keys" to my successful pursuit of The Best of Both Worlds is what I share with you now.

**Individually
these Keys will open the doors to
Happiness, Health, Wealth and Wisdom,
but collectively they will open the gates
to a Kingdom of Limitless Possibilities
and Endless Opportunities!**

Enjoy the ride!

IN OPTIMO CERTE
UTRIUSQUE MUNDI THEORIA

As we traverse
the following lessons and concepts
all that I ask you to bring
is an open mind
a Positive Attitude
and an eagerness to Improve yourself

For without these
you cannot grow

**There is
a better way
to live your life**

**and it is achieved
through continuous
and never-ending
Self-Improvement**

Your Body, Mind and Soul are the starting points of all Self-Improvement

Cultivate Your Mind
Optimize Your Health
Satisfy Your Soul!

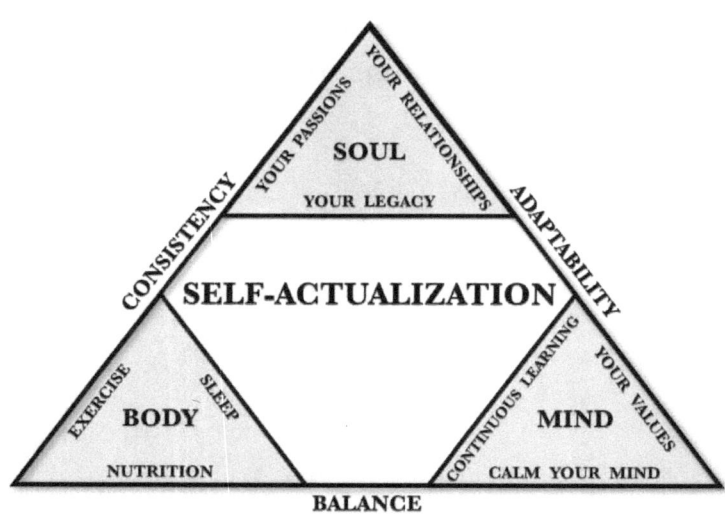

The Self-Actualization Pyramid
by: Eric J. Safranek

Take the time
to define
and put on paper
the person that you aspire
to evolve into

Then take the required steps you need
to become one
with your ideal

**Improvement
begins
with
a
single
Decision**

**You must learn how
to specifically define
exactly what it is
that you intend to bring
into your life**

**Strive to discover
your Purpose
and your Passion
as well as the Path
that you are destined to follow**

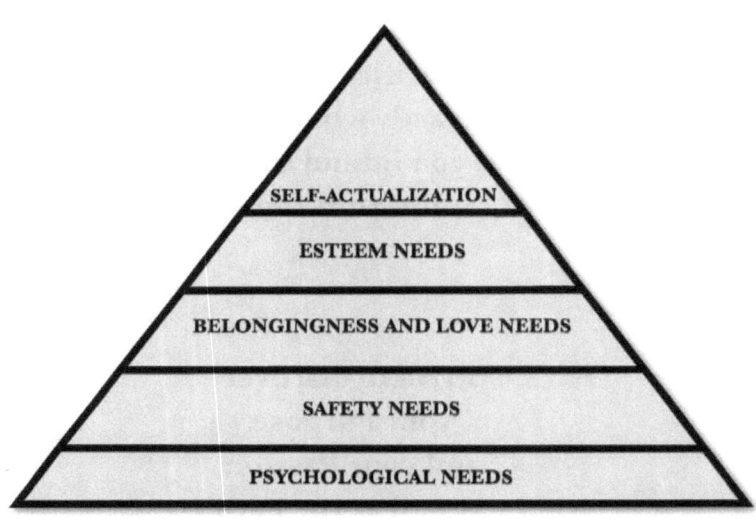

Maslow's Hierarchy of Needs

SELF-ACTUALIZATION

"A Musician must make Music,
an Artist must Paint,
a Poet must Write,
if he is to be ultimately at peace with himself.

What a man can be, he must be.
He must be true to his own nature.
This need we may call self-actualization...

It refers to man's desire for self-fulfillment, namely,
to the tendency for him to become actualized in
what he is potentially.
This tendency might be phrased as
the desire to become more and more what one
idiosyncratically is,

to become everything
that one is capable of becoming."

–Abraham Maslow, from the book
Motivation and Personality

INFINITE LOOPS
OF PERPETUAL HAPPINESS

**Success and Joy
can be found intertwined
amongst
Infinite Loops
of Perpetual Happiness**

Infinite Loops of Perpetual Happiness

Seek out those,
"A-ha!"
epiphanies
and moments of realization
that alter and recalibrate
the compass
of your everyday life

Infinite Loops of Perpetual Happiness are created when the actions you take feed off one another. For example, take a look at my personal Infinite Loop of Exercise:

The more Exercise I get, the more Energy I have.
The more Energy I have,
the more productive I am.
The more productive I am, the better I feel.
The better I feel, the more I Exercise...

And so, an Infinite Loop of Perpetual Happiness is formed!

Little by little I got healthier and healthier over the years. As I became more comfortable within my new skin, my confidence soared. As my confidence and appearance improved, the more people started to notice me. The more attention I received, the more I chose to improve myself.

**Take time away
from your normal routine**

**Perform all of the
essential physical improvements
and daily mental maintenance
required to achieve
all the small victories
and magnificent accomplishments
of your enduring Legacy**

Two of my greatest Passions in life are Learning and Traveling. Notice how I am able to feed one off another:

The more I write, the more I research.
The more I research, the more I learn.
The more places that I learn about,
the more I travel.
The more I travel, the more I learn and discover.
The more I learn and discover,
the more I research.
The more I research, the more I write.
The more I write, the more I earn.
The more I earn, the more I travel,
The more I travel, the more I write...
And so... another Infinite Loop of Perpetual
Happiness is formed!

Writing allows me the flexibility I need to write about whatever it is that I am interested in at that specific moment. I research it, then get to share my ideas with the world. Writing allows me the flexibility I need to live and work anywhere in the World!

SECTION II

OPTIMIZE YOUR HEALTH

A HEALTHY BODY

**All that ails you
and all that heals you
emanates from within**

No matter of its condition today
or what you've done in the past
you must make the efforts
to maintain your Health
in order to continue
your journey through
this wonderful thing
called life

Your body
is the one and only vessel you have
to carry you through
this lifelong voyage

Constantly repair your body
Improve your body
and Adapt to your body's changes

TOBACCO

If you use tobacco, in any form, stop right now. Do not fall victim to new attempts in repackaging or rebranding, for it is a drug with no benefit, only consequences.

To receive help with a Smoking addiction, visit:
www.smokefree.gov

DRUGS

If you use illegal narcotics, hallucinogens or hard drugs, seek treatment immediately and receive the help you need to conquer your addictions. No matter the circumstances that lead to your usage, help is available and begins the moment you admit you have a problem.

To receive help with a Drug addiction, visit:
www.na.org

ALCOHOL

If you drink alcohol, do so in moderation. According to general census, it appears that most women may safely consume one drink per day and men may have one or two per day... but not every day...

You must give your liver a few days off per week and longer stints throughout the year. Keep in mind that **abstaining is by far the best recommendation**. If you are an Alcoholic or have a hereditary disposition to Alcoholism, then you must avoid alcohol completely and seek the support you need to treat this socially acceptable drug, yet deceiving disease.

To receive help with an Alcohol addiction, visit:

www.aa.org

MARAJUANA

At this point I will neither endorse nor discourage marijuana use. I believe that marijuana has many legitimate medical uses and can truly help thousands of people that are fighting pain, seizures and other illnesses. I also believe that the occasional joint here or there could possibly assist some adults in relaxing or even increasing their creativity.

I believe that non-THC hemp is an excellent renewable resource that we should be utilizing in the production of paper products, clothing and other industrial uses. And I also believe that marijuana has gone through well over fifty years of testing, (compared to the limited six to twenty-four months that most prescription drugs receive) and scrutiny without conclusive proof of major long term effects or side effects worse than our number one acceptable drug... alcohol.

The studies and information available are often conflicting, deceiving and biased. Unfortunately nowadays, if you follow the money, you can usually predict the results...

Balance is Key. You do not want to go through life in a haze. If you rely upon it for a legitimate or severe medical condition, then minimal use may be appropriate. If you use marijuana on a daily basis simply for recreation or an unfounded medical condition that you use to justify your usage, then you are abusing the drug and need to deal with your addiction.

To receive help with a Marijuana addiction, visit:
www.marijuana-anonymous.org

DEPRESSION

For those families, spouses and friends that are dealing with a loved one's depression and addictions, proceed with the utmost of Patience, Love and resiliency. Though you cannot help someone who does not want help, you can always remain faithfully by their side, patiently waiting for that moment of epiphany that inspires them to quit or that moment of hitting rock bottom when they need you the most. Unfortunately, there is not a simple singular solution to help those that suffer from depression and addiction. Often several different approaches and attempts are necessary along the path to recovery.

NEVER GIVE UP and never surrender to what may seem like unsurmountable obstacles in your life. If you're thinking of harming yourself or others, please seek out help **IMMEDIATELY**!

To receive help, visit:
The National Suicide Prevention Lifeline
1-800-273-8255 (within the U.S.)
www.suicidepreventionlifeline.org

PRESCRIPTION & OTC DRUGS

And finally, what I believe to be the greatest threat in the drug world... Prescription Drugs, Pharmaceuticals and OTC, (Over The Counter) drugs. This is where I need to reiterate that I am NOT a Medical Doctor. This is also where I should tell you to go see your Doctor for proper medical advice. I am reluctant because of the influence of the Pharmaceutical Industry upon the Medical Profession and the lack of natural and nutritional advice that doctors prescribe.

What I will suggest is that you speak to both a Doctor AND a Nutritionist, then do your own research. Do not search for a miracle pill when a natural cure is available. **Embrace and search for Natural Cures.** It is my belief that of the many diseases that plague us throughout our lifetimes, a majority of them are preventable or curable by exercise and proper nutrition alone.

Seek out non-drug treatments whenever possible as many of the drugs used to treat depression, often have suicidal side effects either while taking or soon after discontinuing. Look into therapy, lifestyle changes and other natural or holistic remedies first. Use depression medications only as a last resort and when prescribed and under the close supervision of a physician and/or therapist.

To receive help with a
Prescription Drug addiction, visit:

www.na.org

Discover your Balance
between modern medicines and
Natural Cures

Remember what Hippocrates,
the "Father of Modern Medicine" said,
so many centuries ago:

*"Let food be thy medicine,
and medicine be thy food."*

NUTRITION

*"You can't exercise your way
out of a bad diet"*

-Mark Hyman

**Through modernization,
urbanization and
industrialization
We have sacrificed the quality of our food
for Corporate profits
and convenience**

**The key to better health
lies in the quality of food
that we introduce into our body**

In a world that is filled with such polarizing extremes and an all-or-nothing attitude, perhaps a better approach would be celebrating small victories and following the tortoise's advice: slow and steady wins the race.

**Once we realize that
Real Foods
with their natural fats and sugars
are healthier than the
manufactured and refined
chemical experiments
that we currently consume,
can we then start to lay the foundations
of a healthier lifestyle**

THE REAL FOOD DIET

The Real Food Diet is not actually a diet, but instead a permanent lifestyle change and new approach to eating that focuses upon a few basic concepts: Education, Honesty and Non-Processed Foods, such as fruits and vegetables.

The Real Food Diet simply stated:

Eat less of what is bad for you and more of what is good for you

Drastic diet changes seldom become new habits. But, what if you could gradually add more nutritious foods to your existing diet and strategically start making better decisions week to week? Can you go one day without fast food or a soda this week? Can you dedicate one day next week to eating Vegetarian? What about two days? Can you get to the point where you can consistently commit one full day each week to juicing or eating exclusively Organic Vegan food?

With such an abundance of knowledge and information it is your primary duty to do your own research and determine what makes sense and works for you. You must make the effort to become aware of the toxic foods that are hurting you and the healthy options, (not just fads and trends) which exist, that can help you heal your own body. Once you select the foods that you should be eating, it becomes your responsibility to monitor yourself. Simply start by adding better foods to your existing diet and then expanding your repertoire of healthy options from there.

**The better your determination is
between good foods and bad foods
the better your results will be**

**The more often you choose
higher quality foods and
healthier cooking options
the better your results will be**

**The more honest you are with yourself
THE BETTER YOUR RESULTS WILL BE!**

Now let's be completely honest with each other for just a moment...

**Deep down inside
we all know what is actually good for us
and attempt to justify
what is bad for us**

Portion control is one of the fundamental problems with the American Diet. You must invest the time in reeducating yourself on portion size. The amount of food that we currently serve, eat and discard per person is ridiculously out of line with those of other advanced countries.

Balance is Key

You can **thrive and survive** on a lot less food than you are conditioned to believe. All too often we mistake hunger pangs as a craving for comfort food, when in actuality, what our body truly desires is **more nutritious foods**.

THE REAL FOOD ENEMIES

Processed Foods

Carcinogenic Foods

Diet Foods

GMOs

Sodas

Excess Sugar

Artificial Coloring

Artificial Flavoring

Artificial Sweeteners

Meats raised with hormones and antibiotics

Non-organic foods laced with excessive fertilizers

GENERALIZED GUIDELINES FOR THE REAL FOOD DIET

Avoid sugary foods and drinks as well as artificial sweeteners and high fructose corn syrup.

Beware of diet, reduced-fat and low-fat foods.

EAT REAL FOODS! Foods that consist of just one ingredient.

DRINK MORE WATER! Start your day off with one to three glasses of fresh clean water upon waking to cleanse and rehydrate your body. Continually drink water throughout the day to stay properly hydrated and remove the toxins from your body.

Choose to eat Fresh Raw, (or slightly streamed) Organic Vegetables whenever possible and avoid the deep fryer.

Choose Homemade or Freshly Prepared Foods over Processed or Pre-packaged foods. If you want lasagna, the one you make at home will most likely be healthier than the one you purchase in the frozen foods aisle.

The Nutrition you receive
from the foods that you eat
can either strengthen your immune system
or weaken and make it prone
to illness and disease

The choice is yours

**The more chemicals you put
in and on your body
the more toxins
your body
must attempt to remove**

For right now, I will withhold my opinion of current Cancer treatments and practices. I will however, suggest that you check out
Ty Bollinger's website, "The Truth About Cancer" in order to learn more about alternative treatments and the options that are available to you as well as some lifestyle changes that you can make today in an attempt to lower your risk of Cancer.

www.TheTruthAboutCancer.com

Your body
is a Self-Healing
Conscious
and Subconsciously controlled,
regenerative organism
that is fueled by
oxygen, water and nutrients

A body that receives
clean Air
filtered Water
and Healthy Nutritious foods
will be able to
wage the greatest wars against disease
and make the most expeditious repairs
to an ill or injured body

Pay no attention
to the negative thoughts and voices
inside your head

Instead...
Listen to your gut
Listen to your moods
Listen to your emotions

Learn to listen to your body
for it is forever attempting
to let you know
when you are getting too much
or too little
of a good
or bad thing

EXERCISE

**"Regular Exercise
can reduce pain,
stress,
and blood pressure
while also
fighting depression,
increasing Energy,
improving Strength,
and boosting Self-Esteem"**

–from the book,
Happy, Healthy, Wealthy & Wise

Consistency
is
Key

Sporadic attempts
yield weak results

Consistent Actions
produce new behaviors

The next Key towards improving your Health is to just **GET MOVING**! Take the stairs, park further away, walk your dog, go for a bike ride, or just simply go for a walk. Go outside and get some fresh air. Walking is easily the single best exercise that I know of to begin your journey towards better health. As you progress, you can gradually add inclines, terrain, interval jogging and sprinting into the mix. If it is snowing outside, then shovel snow. If it is raining, then walk or jog in place inside your home and go for a walk later.

"Movement is Life"

–from the movie,
World War Z

Your Health
is
Your Priority

The goal here isn't to look like Arnold Schwarzenegger, but instead to tone your muscles and improve your strength. By adding weight training to your workouts a couple times a week, you will strengthen your bones, improve your balance, burn calories more efficiently and improve your overall health. You can use free weights, universal exercise machines or even perform basic push-ups, pull-ups and squats.

Remember, as Isaac Newton once stated, "An object that is at rest will stay at rest." My advice to you is: keep moving, because a body in motion will stay in motion. If a majority of your waking hours are spent sitting at work then inactively watching TV at home, do not pretend to be surprised by the excess weight you carry around with you or your overall lack of energy. Your body requires more exercise then simply walking back and forth to the car or bathroom. The more you move today, the more energy you will have tomorrow.

When you can't
you must
When you stand still
you rust

The best exercise
is the one you enjoy
and perform
most consistently

We are given 1,440 minutes each and every day to do anything we choose.

You only need to dedicate but twenty minutes of cardio each day to maintain your Health and an additional twenty to forty minutes every other day of additional cardio, weights and/or strength training, to Improve your Health.

There are thousands of books and videos out there explaining different exercises, machines and routines. Which is the best? If you like walking, then walk. If you prefer running, then run. If you prefer machines over free weights, then choose the one that you will do consistently and not dread.

Do not limit your workouts to the confines of a gym. Remember exercise should be fun and you can receive the same benefits of exercise by simply playing with your kids, playing with your dog, cleaning the house or best of all...
having Sex!

SLEEP

"Sleep is the best Meditation"

–The Dalai Lama

Sleep... simply the most rewarding, underutilized and least appreciated key to your health. A good night's sleep is known to: improve Memory, increase Creativity, boost brain function, lower stress, strengthen your immune system, reduce inflammation, improve alertness, and may even help you live longer! Adults should aim for seven to nine hours of sleep every night.

When you are sick, aching or lethargic, it is often due to a lack of proper sleep. All too often we reach for some aspirin or other over-the-counter drug to rid ourselves of a simple headache or mild pain while simply avoiding the common sense approach of:

Water – to rehydrate and detoxify your body
Exercise – taking a brisk walk outside in fresh air
Rest – to allow your body proper time to recover

Even less respected in our hectic adult lives than sleep, is napping. Taking a short break from your busy day will pay you back exponentially! Taking short naps of five to twenty-five minutes can: Improve your alertness, productivity, Creativity, Concentration, elevate your mood, and sharpen your motor skills.

Adults should be sure to keep their naps under 45 minutes in order to avoid changes to their sleep cycle.

**Learn to appreciate
periods of Rest & Relaxation
every single day
and enjoy all the benefits
of waking up
Refreshed
Renewed
and
Refocused**

Be sure to have pen and paper available as you nap or sleep. Be on the lookout for flashes of insight, as these frequently offer the signposts you seek in progressing your everyday life. Do not be quick to dismiss what may first appear to be a tangent thought. Often this thought is guiding you to see either a new path or an unseen angle.

SECTION III

CULTIVATE YOUR MIND

A BEAUTIFUL MIND

"A man's mind may be likened to a garden,
which may be intelligently cultivated
or allowed to run wild...

Just as a gardener cultivates his plot...

so may a man
tend to the garden of his mind,
weeding out all the wrong,
useless, and impure thoughts,
and cultivating toward perfection
the flowers and fruits of right,
useful, and pure thoughts. "

–James Allen, from the book
As A Man Thinketh

**Take the time to
improve your mind
and your attitudes
for they alone
are forever formulating
your potential Happiness
and perceived reality**

To improve your life
you must
Improve
your
Thoughts

Meditation calms the mind,
Sleep rejuvenates the mind,
Water hydrates the mind,
books nourish the mind,
Visualizations exercise the mind
and your Morals guide the mind

Your Beliefs
define
your life

We each personally possess the power to improve any area of our life and create the life we seek.

**We all carry within us
an evolutionary frontal lobe
unlike that of any other animal on Earth**

**This frontal lobe allows us to
rehearse future events
before they even happen**

**We can practice
without the sweat
We can study
without the books**

CALM YOUR MIND

**Meditation
is the means by which
you reconnect your Soul
to the Infinite Wisdom
of the Universe**

Become the peaceful Calm
within the eye of the storm

Generate an impenetrable force field
of Positive Energy
that ceaselessly surrounds you
and inundates your mind
with Powerful Thoughts

Those that do not have
the time to Meditate
are usually the ones
that need it the most

Meditation is like
praying to the Universe

It reconnects you
to an infinite bank of
Knowledge
Serenity
and Possibilities

We see
what we want
to see

If you are generally a Happy
and Positive person
you will encounter
many
Positive
outcomes

If you are generally a negative
or pessimistic person
you will see
only what is wrong
instead of
what is possible

Learn to live
harmoniously and in sync
amongst Both your inner
and outer Worlds

Your interpretation
of the outside World
is controlled
from within

Unfortunately
far too many people
unknowingly give away
much of their power
and allow outside stimuli
to alter their Thoughts
their Health
and their Physiology

**Daily Motivation
is the
Key to Achievement
and
Continued Success**

ALIGNED CONFIDENCE
What I think about
what I choose to Focus upon
what I truly Believe
the Actions I take
and my Inner Dialogue
ALL must be Aligned

COMPLETE & TOTAL CONFIDENCE
Without Doubt
Without Fear
Without Worry
I know what I am doing is right
I Know I Will Succeed!

Pursue
  Improvement
  Not

                              perFection

For what is perfection
but an impossible benchmark to reach

ADVICE FROM
A RECOVERING PERFECTIONIST

Perfection is an unattainable goal. The mere search for a perfect mate, perfect job or perfect life is within itself a flawed pursuit as it will in turn become a pursuit to elicit imperfections. Instead, decide to **Enjoy Perfect Moments!**

That mesmerizing sunset, an acknowledged success or brief moment of intimate bliss. Acknowledging and Focusing upon these will bring even more Perfect Moments into your life!

DEFINE YOUR VALUES

"Your Beliefs become your thoughts,
Your thoughts become your words,
Your words become your Actions,
Your Actions become your habits,
Your habits become your Values,
Your Values become your Destiny"

–Mahatma Gandhi

THE GOLDEN RULE

*"Do unto others
as you would have them
do unto you."*

–Matthew 7:12

THE GOLDEN MEAN

*"The desirable middle
between two extremes,
one of excess
and the other
of deficiency."*

–Aristotle

THE MIDDLE WAY

**Seek not to live in extremities
but instead establish
your own
perfect
--- BALANCE ---**

*"Make your Attitudes
your Allies"*

–David J. Schwartz, from the book
The Magic of Thinking Big

I am
Happy, Healthy, Wealthy & Wise!

I am
Positive, Confident, Focused, ENERGÍA!

I am Happy
I am Healthy
I am Wealthy
I am Wise

I am Positive
I am Confident
I am Focused
I am..... ENERGÍA!

TRANSITION YOUR POSSIBILITIES
INTO BELIEF

**For as long as you invite doubt
into your mind
it constantly remains
as a fallback excuse
for short term defeat**

**Never allow
a negative thought
to sabotage your Confidence
or Passionate Pursuit**

The goal here is to eventually get to the point where you can honestly say:

**I Know
What I Am Doing
Is Right,
I KNOW
I WILL
SUCCEED!**

**The more people
that I personally connect to**

**the more rewarding
my life will be!**

I will always be led down the correct path
if I simply follow my gut instincts
and consistently make decisions
that Align with my Morals

**Strive to be
the Positive and Energetic person
that people like to be around...
it's contagious!**

"Every day,
in every way,
I am getting better and better"

"I have never cured anyone in my life.
All I do is show people
how they can cure themselves."

–Émile Coué

Every day
in every way
I'm getting
Better & Better
Healthier & Healthier
Smarter & Smarter
Richer & Richer!

SEE it - FEEL it - BELIEVE it

SEE it in your Mind
FEEL it in your Soul
BELIEVE it in your Heart

MEDITATE – MOTIVATE
EXERCISE – VISUALIZE

Meditate – I will Calm my mind and constantly refocus throughout the day!

Motivate – I will Motivate myself and build my Confidence every single morning!

Exercise – I will Improve my Health and increase my ENEGÍA every single day!

Visualize – I will Visualize living the Lifestyle that I am destined to live! I water the seeds of success every single day!

Build your Confidence
and increase your Focus
to squash out any
doubts
worries
and fears
that may enter your mind

"More wars have been waged
within the mind of men,
then ever fought
upon any battlefield."

–Unknown

All too often
we justify our fears
and fuel our doubts

Never allow doubt
to enter your mind
for what is doubt
but self-sabotage

This internal terrorism
that we allow to occur
has destroyed more dreams
than any other stimuli

"If you want others to be happy,
practice Compassion.

If you want to be happy,
practice Compassion."

–The Dalai Lama

Allow yourself to be Happy!

**Do not allow
loss
pain
or regret
to prevent you from obtaining
the joy that you seek**

**Give yourself permission
to enjoy the life
that you so righteously deserve**

CONTINUE YOUR EDUCATION

**A Continuous
Unconventional
Never-Ending
Pursuit
For Knowledge**

We
as a society
have lost touch
with our basic
mental and cognitive muscles
including but not limited to:

Memory
Decision
Contemplation
Creativity
Mindfulness
Focus
Reasoning
and overall
Quantitative Literacy

We therefore must make the efforts
and take the necessary steps
to retrain
our Brain

Once you have received a basic Education, it becomes your personal responsibility to continue your lifelong Education through both conventional AND unconventional means.

Nowadays, armed only with an internet connection, you can access a World Wide Database of free and minimal cost educational tools. Open your mind to learn from as many different schools of thought as possible from the widest array of people all over the World. For there is not a single person on this Earth that we cannot learn from.

The inconvenient truth with Education is that it makes you less ignorant. You sacrifice your innocence and ignorance for intelligence.

Ignorance WAS bliss
but now that you know
what you know
you must continue through
the remainder of your life
eating Healthier
utilizing a more prodigious vocabulary
and questioning dogma

Through the lessons you learn
the people you meet
the conversations you share
and the Memorable Experiences
you shall encounter
there is no better teacher in the World
than Travel

As your Experiences multiply
your horizons expand
and your World View grows

(Life × Experiences) + Knowledge² = Perspective³

*"If you talk to a man
in a language he understands,
that goes to his head.
If you talk to him in his own language,
that goes to his heart."*

–Nelson Mandela

By learning a new language, you not only communicate and better understand others and their culture, but will forever view your native culture in a whole new light. The more languages you learn, the more people you can communicate with.

**For each language you learn,
your World grows exponentially**

**Improved Self-Image
will always precede
a fit body**

**For beauty cannot exist
before you acknowledge it**

My thoughts and Beliefs
create the physical World
all around me

They direct every single
Experience, Emotion, Sensation,
Memory and Lesson
that I will ever learn

Everything I see, hear, feel, smell and taste

Everything I enjoy
and all the beauty in the World
is a result of
my own
personal
perceptions

Once you fully understand and accept this
concept you will better comprehend how all the
Improvements in your life actually stem from a
Single Decisive Thought.

*"Unfortunately, no one can be told
what the Matrix is.
You have to see it for yourself...*

*You are a slave, Neo.
Like everyone else you were born into bondage.
Into a prison that you cannot taste or see or touch.
A prison for your mind...*

*I'm trying to free your mind, Neo.
But I can only show you the door.
You're the one that has to walk through it...*

*This is your last chance.
After this, there is no turning back.
You take the blue pill - the story ends,
you wake up in your bed and believe
whatever you want to believe.
You take the red pill - you stay in Wonderland
and I show you how deep
the rabbit-hole goes."*

–from the movie
The Matrix

MIND POWER

**Thinking has simultaneously become
my greatest enemy
as well as
my greatest ally**

I am still fighting who I was
in
an
attempt
to become
the person I can be

While some changes are immediate, others take time. Learn to expect random and unexpected changes, (such as a job offer out of the blue) and develop the patience for slower changes to transpire, (such as losing weight.)

Learn to respond...

Instead of react

**Mind Control
is simply a skill to be developed
in order to Calm Your Mind
during times of restlessness
and boost your ENERGÍA
during times of apathy**

"You can change your life in an instant
by simply changing your thinking.

YOUR life is based upon
YOUR communication
with YOURSELF.
You create YOUR world.
Your beliefs are what decide YOUR
Happiness
Success
Accomplishments
and Reality.

Positive Thoughts
open both the mind and the eyes to see
what a negative mind cannot."

–from the book,
Happy, Healthy, Wealthy & Wise

Quiet your Mind
Command your Thoughts
Direct your Life

Remember...
You are
the Writer
the Director
the Producer and
the Leading Actor
of your everyday life

Discover your Inspiration
Conceive your ideal character
Collaborate with the best cast and crew
And give the performance of a lifetime!

PROBLEM... SOLUTION

Fear, guilt, depression, anxiety and anger may offer the motivation you need to change but not the solutions you are searching for to the challenges that you face.

Whenever you allow fear, worry, doubt and negative thoughts to slip into your consciousness, you distract yourself from discovering a successful solution to your problem.

The question is not WHY is this happening to me, but instead, **WHAT can I do Right Now to resolve this problem?** Learn to Focus your Energy upon a successful solution instead of the problem itself.

The question is not WHY
The question is WHAT
The answer is HOW

"The body is the servant of the mind...

Disease and Health... are rooted in thought...

There is no physician like cheerful thought for dissipating the ills of the body"

–James Allen, from the book
As a Man Thinketh

THE PLACEBO PROOF

I can prove, beyond a reasonable doubt that a mind-body connection exists. Even if you do not believe a word I write or any of the hundreds of other books written on mind-body connection, I hope that you believe in the Sciences that have been proving it for decades amongst thousands of experiments all over the world. The proof of course I am referring to is The Placebo Effect.

The Placebo Effect: a beneficial effect, produced by a placebo drug or treatment, that cannot be attributed to the placebo itself but instead to a patient's beliefs and expectations of said treatment.

The Nocebo Response: a negative effect, produced by a drug or treatment, unrelated to the specific properties of the treatment that is a result of conscious or subconscious beliefs and expectations.

Where a placebo increases a patient's Health through conscious thoughts, a nocebo decreases a patient's health through subconscious beliefs and negative conditioning. These two regularly occurring events, offer further proof of the mind-body connection and just how important it is to positively focus upon healing your own body.

The correlation between what the Doctor advises and what is experienced by the patient is in direct relation to the perceived expectations of the patient. What this tells us is twofold:

A) A patient's beliefs can affect the outcome of a procedure, drug or treatment. The stronger your beliefs and expectations in a treatment, the more likely you are to see those results materialize.

B) A Doctor's advice can effectively help or hurt a patient's treatment. Make sure to use an optimistic Doctor that truly believes in his ability to cure, (not just treat) you.

There are additional studies out there that further justify the mind-body connection which go on to prove what a Doctor believes is also transferred to the patient, meaning that if the Doctor does not believe a drug will help or that it actually is a placebo, the patient's body will not respond to said treatment.

It simply comes down to a patient's belief in that treatment and the expectations delivered to the patient by the doctor. The stronger the belief, the more likely it is that a person will experience what they expect.

We are all sponges that absorb and feed off the energy of the people all around us. So be careful in choosing the people which you surround yourself with.

Positive people attract positive outcomes
while negative people attract negative outcomes.
Like attracts like, for this is the Law of Attraction.

Everything happening right now is a result of your past thinking and actions. The best approach to improving your future is to start taking positive steps in the right direction, instead of focusing upon the mistakes of the past.

You control your own future, so remember:

**Each positive step you take today
will pay dividends tomorrow**

**There are some people that become
such Positive and powerful energy magnets
that you can feel their good Energy
the moment they walk into a room**

**Some call it Karma,
some call it Aura,
I call it ENERGÍA!**

These people are producing so much positive energy and good vibrations that they have enough to share with others, which in turn, surrounds themselves with similar people that reciprocate and send them even more positive energy right back.

And so another
Infinite Loop of Perpetual Happiness
is created!

121

EXPAND YOUR THINKING

*"Education is the most powerful weapon
which you can use
to change the World."*

–Nelson Mandela

*"The only thing that interferes with my learning
is my Education."*

–Albert Einstein

"End the Delusion of Time...
The past gives you an identity
and the future holds the promise of salvation...
both are Illusions."

–Eckhart Tolle, from the book
The Power of Now

Most humans
cannot truly fathom
or fully comprehend
time, size, distance
or just how connected we actually are
to each and every particle
within the known Universe

Time is a remarkably infallible teacher

It lends us the perspective we need
the distance to heal
and constantly serves as a reminder
of lessons already learned

Time allows for Contemplation;
Contemplation leads to Perspective;
Perspective stimulates Inspiration

*"If you want to find
the secrets of the Universe,
think in terms of
Energy,
Frequency
and Vibration."*

–Nikola Tesla

It is my belief that there is an Energy
which we have yet to measure

A frequency too high or too low
for us to sense

A vibration that most
have yet to correctly identify

One of which that connects
every single one of us
to every single
being
organism
and atom
within the known Universe

"If your religion is an important part of your life, than I am Happy for you without regard for which religion it is. As far as different religions are concerned, to me they're just different paths leading to the same place. A thousand paths to a single destination."

–Willie Nelson, from the book
The Tao of Willie

**If you are religious,
then you may believe
that God exists within you**

**If you are of a scientific mind
you may believe
that the very matter
which originated from the Big Bang
is within us all**

**Either way you must agree...
WE ARE ALL CONNECTED!**

"The kingdom of God is within you"

–Luke 17:21

If your faith makes you feel good
gives you the guidance you need
and a sense of community
then I strongly encourage you
to follow your faith

If you or one of your religious leaders
interpret your religion
in a way that promotes
hatred, killing
or values that are out-of-line
with your true beliefs,
then I emphatically recommend
that you question your faith
and loyalty to it

What if...

**The person you hope to be
is someone you already were
and strive to become again?**

Imagine for a moment...

That either in a past life
or an alternate Universe
you have already lived the life
that you are currently pursing
and already possess
all the
Tools
Training
and Confidence
to do it all over again

Perpetually Pursue your life
with the utmost Confidence
and Vigor!

SECTION IV

SATISFY YOUR SOUL

A PASSIONATE SOUL

"Happiness resides not in possessions,
and not in gold,
Happiness dwells in the soul"

–Democritus

"Find out who you are and be that person.
That's what your Soul was put on this Earth to be.
Find that truth, live that truth
and everything else will come."

–Ellen DeGeneres

YOUR PASSIONS

"Well there comes a time
when it's either this or death.

I'm not gonna try to do anything else,
I'm gonna die trying to do this...

You don't have life,
if you don't have a dream"

–Morgan Freeman

"**Discover your Passions in**
Work
Life
and
Love
and you shall unearth
your Path to Happiness."

–from the book,
Happy, Healthy, Wealthy & Wise

**Continually strive
to improve your Focus
and share your Passionate Soul
with the World!**

Always remain flexible and open-minded for the initial goal that you originally set out upon may only have been one of training for something bigger and better than you ever could have imagined.

For you may be thrust upon a path which spawns an accomplishment that shatters the shackles of our preexisting beliefs and destroys the bonds of our previously limited realm of possibilities.

**Specifically define your Passion
then broadly pursue a Path towards it**

**A lack of decision
is a choice**

                        **and therefore
a decision within itself**

THREE QUESTIONS

What do I want to do with my life?

What am I most Passionate about?

**What sort of Legacy
do I wish to bestow
upon the World?**

"Your work is going to fill a large part of your life, and the only way to be truly satisfied is to do what you believe is great work. And the only way to do great work is to love what you do. If you haven't found it yet, keep looking. Don't settle. As with all matters of the heart, you'll know when you find it. And, like any great relationship, it just gets better and better as the years roll on. So keep looking until you find it. Don't settle."

–Steve Jobs
Stanford Commencement Speech
June 2005

HOW TO IDENTIFY YOUR PASSION

1) Make a list of things that you are Intensely Interested in.

2) Look for patterns and trends. What general categories would you arrange your interests into?

3) Specifically Define, EXACTLY what it is, that you want out of life. What are you looking for in Life, Love and Career? What type of Lifestyle do you see yourself living? If money were no object, where would you go and what would you do? What type of people would you surround yourself with?

4) Contemplate your life with the end in mind. What will be your Legacy? What will you be remembered for? How many lives will you have affected for the better?

5) Start building your Legacy today and doing what interests you most. Though ultimately nothing on your list may transform in to your true Passion or Purpose in life, this will at least start you off along a pathway of discovery.

**Specifically define your
Lifestyle Goals
Livelihood Goals
and Legacy Goals**

**Set incremental goals
and completion dates for each**

Look for the signposts
along the path of life
as they will be disguised as
interests
mistakes
failures
opportunities
chance encounters
flashes of insight
and the forks in the road
of your everyday life

What is the
ONE
CENTRAL
PURPOSE
that consumes your thoughts
and Energizes your life?

I believe that we are all here on this planet for a reason. **EVERY SINGLE PERSON** has something to contribute. Some of us go on to live negative lives or leave a nightmarish legacy behind, while most of us strive to live a more positive life and do good things for the ones we cherish most. We cannot comprehend why some people are so evil. I personally believe that all actions, both good and bad, direct our society as a whole.

**While some people motivate us
by the good deeds they do
others shall serve as warnings
as to the development and direction
of all Humanity**

YOUR RELATIONSHIPS

"Women marry men hoping they will change.
Men marry women hoping they will not.
So each is inevitably disappointed."

–Albert Einstein

"Some people ask the secret of our long marriage.
We take the time to go to a restaurant
two times a week.
A little candlelight, dinner,
soft music and dancing.
She goes Tuesdays,
I go Fridays."

–Henry Youngman

One of the top regrets held by Centurions and those on their death bed is not spending enough time with family and friends. Every single day that we walk this Earth is yet another opportunity to expand our circle of friends and improve our current relationships. Once you are willing to change your approach and improve yourself, you will see that the opportunities for friendship are limitless. At a very basic level, people want to connect to others and be understood. So it is up to you to go above and beyond to enhance your relationships. Do not keep score of who called whom last. If you think of an old friend or family member you haven't spoken to in a while, be the bigger person and the one to reach out first. More than likely, they will welcome your conversation because as I said before, people instinctively desire to Develop Profound Personal Connections with other people.

Make it your job to connect to as many people as you can throughout your lifetime. Remember, I said connect, not collect – as we do with Facebook friends. I am talking about making a real connection with another human whether it is through common goals, beliefs or an amazing conversation.

**Continually improve upon
and expand your network
of competent business professionals
true Friends
and loving Family**

Focus your attention to those relationships that benefit you most – positive and supporting relationships. Do your best to avoid or minimize negative or harmful relationships and those people that do not have your best interests in mind. In other words... SURROUND YOURSELF WITH THE RIGHT PEOPLE.

**As you take the time to listen
and share great conversation
the lines become blurred
between who is helping who**

The time you invest in sharing memorable conversations with a friend, family member or stranger, will pay dividends exponentially and create a Positive Domino Effect within the life of both participants. We all have issues and struggles within our lives. We all need to vent. We all just want to be understood. And all too often, an ear will help more than a hand.

**As you connect
and relate to more people
you will repeatedly learn
that we are all basically the same**

**We are just humans
seeking Happiness, Purpose and Pleasure
while trying to avoid
pain, death and suffering**

HABITUAL OPTIMISTIC PREJUDICE

Through repetition and practice, you can teach yourself how to become instinctually optimistic by consistently identifying the good, or possibility of good, in each person and situation. Learn to discover potential, hidden talents, and see the basic intentions of other people's actions.

Give people the benefit of the doubt, give them a second chance and do not hold grudges against family. As we learn throughout our life – the power that other people have over us is in direct relation to the amount of focus that we place upon our relationship with them. Concentrate your focus upon the Positive Relationships within your life and either repair or let go of all the detrimental relationships that are holding you back.

*"If you love until it hurts,
there can be no more hurt,
only more love."*

–Mother Teresa

and most importantly... Love!

Love without fear of loss
dependency
or getting hurt

Find a good person
then give everything you've got!

Don't hold back...
Dive right in!

For which is of greater regret:
Caring too much
or Loving too little?

I cannot remember exactly how long into my marriage that this next epiphany occurred. But somewhere along the way I realized why all those relationships from the past never worked out; why I was lonely for so long; and why it took me thirty-seven years to get married. If any of those relationships from my past had worked out or if I had settled on someone less than perfect for me, I never would have met Paula – the love of my life!

Now I do not mean to diminish the feelings I felt for others in the past – I am actually grateful for each and every person that came into my life! Every single relationship that I have had has forged me into a better person. It is only in hindsight that I now see how...

**I had to deal with
my demons from the past
before I could ever
move on to the future**

I whole-heartedly wish to apologize to everyone that I may have hurt, mistreated or drove to counseling. I was not, (at that time) refined enough to be the man, the friend or the relative that they each deserved.

**I was not the person
that I am now...**

**Nor the one
that I shall become
tomorrow**

YOUR LEGACY

"If you would not be forgotten
as soon as you are dead,
either write something worth reading
or do something worth writing."

–Benjamin Franklin

You were born
and you will die

Your Purpose on this Earth
is to make the most of what happens
in between these two events

This is what shall become
your Legacy

**Leave a great Legacy
by practicing what you preach
and sharing what you learn**

**Aim to Improve the life
of everyone around you
and create or contribute
to something that is greater
than yourself**

Set your children up for success
and create a Legacy that will thrive
for years after you perish

Create the life of your dreams
with the end in mind

Reverse engineer your life and
**CONTINUALLY CREATE
A LASTING LEGACY**

You do not have to wait
to be great

Start Right Now
and continue to build your Legacy
from this day forward

No matter of your past
start where you stand

From this moment forward
start living a life
of Self-Improvement
and bettering the world
all around you

For you will discover
that these steps that you take
shall eventually become
the Legacy you leave

A NEW HOPE

**When the World is against you
and you see no way out,
the only way through
be a mind
free of doubt**

Hope is what will give you Strength during times of weakness, Confidence during times of doubt and Courage during times of fear. NEVER LOSE HOPE! For as long as you are alive, you've still got a chance! We have all read story after story of amazing people who faced incredible odds, yet successfully emerged from the abyss, Triumphant! We have been lead to believe an infinite number of things that we were told were supposedly impossible... that is, until somebody disregarded the skeptics, took action, and accomplished the impossible!

"Hope is being able to see that there is light despite all of the darkness."

–Desmond Tutu

THE KEYS TO THE KINGDOM

"Believe in Yourself
Believe in your Dreams
Believe in your Success.

Just as you believe
that ice is cold
and fire is hot
you must believe
that you will Succeed"

–from the book,
Happy, Healthy, Wealthy & Wise

**Envision your ideal
then strive to pursue it
on a daily basis**

Continually discover
and improve upon living
a more
Simple
Efficient
and Balanced life

Simplify your life
Simplify your wardrobe

Somewhere between a monk's robe
and one-hundred pairs of shoes
lies a balance of necessity and style

Though it may be a Goal
that we never quite reach

It shall be along this path
that we soon discover

The Joys of the pursuit
and the gratification
of the Journey

**Your greatest
weaknesses
and challenges
contain the opportunity
to evolve into
your greatest
Motivation**

**"Fear Nothing
Assume Nothing
Question Everything
Accept Change"**

–from the book,
Happy, Healthy, Wealthy & Wise

We are given a gift
each and every day
whether we choose to open it
or not

And that gift
is the opportunity
to live within
the present
and fully experience life
within the moment

¡Live Life en Vivo!

No human is without flaw...

No life without a challenge

As with most conflicts
that may arise
in day-to-day life
I do believe that
both the truth
and the solution
are discovered
somewhere
in-between

Where extremities invite conflict
the center provides solutions

QUALITIES OF A HAPPY, HEALTHY, WEALTHY & WISE LEADER

How well you define and incorporate
the following characteristics
into your life

will determine the quality
of the life you lead
and the Legacy
you shall leave
behind.

**A Happy, Healthy, Wealthy
and Wise Leader is.....**

Adaptable
Appreciative
Balanced
Compassionate
Confident
Consistent
Continuously Educated
Creative
Decisive
Disciplined
Efficient
Full of **ENERGÍA!**
Ethical
Focused
Generous
Creating **Infinite Loops of Perpetual Happiness**
Utilizing the **Law of Attraction**
Motivated
Optimistic
Passionate
Patient
Persistent
Respectful
Rested, Relaxed & Rejuvenated
Striving for **Self-Actualization**
Constantly seeking out **Self-Improvement**
Searching for **Simplicity**

So as I awoke this morning to Sonny & Cher's, "I Got You Babe" I wondered for just a moment if I had slipped into a Space–Time Continuum Loop that forced me to live the same day over and over again, year after year. Then I realized that I was living this life by choice, not by chance, and that all along I had possessed the power to alter the redundancy within my own life at any moment had I just fearlessly accepted change and took more action to create the life that I had envisioned.

MANY TALK
FEW **ACT...**

The greatest difference between a successful person and an unsuccessful person is not intelligence, education, luck or skill, but **ACTION!** You could be the smartest guy in the room, with the most training and best business plan, but you will always lose to the person who consistently faces his fears and takes coordinated steps along with **MASSIVE ACTION!**

"Action Cures Fear!"

–David J. Schwartz, from the book
The Magic of Thinking Big

Both Success and failure
are simply temporary moments in time

We may falsely attempt
to designate events
or periods within our lives
as Success or failure
instead of recognizing that life
is simply a series of moments
which you can either live or label

Life is a long road
filled with Profound Peaks
and vast valleys

SUCCESS MOUNTAIN

Visualize for just a moment,
climbing up a steep mountain...
Success Mountain.....

It is a long and strenuous journey.
The view keeps improving, all the way up,
(if you happen to notice it.)
Then you finally reach the peak!

You enjoy the moment,
and try to take it all in.

Unfortunately, due to the thin air
you cannot live upon the peak,
and must continue along your Journey,
because after all, it is a peak, not a plateau.

As you begin cascading down
the opposite side of the mountain,
everything seems easier and less stressful.
You are still elated about your accomplishment
and basking in its glory.

As you continue to descend down
upon the mountain
you sometimes, (but not always)
will have an obvious departure point
and have to make a choice:

Shall I walk on boring, average,
flat ground for a while
or...
Continue the easy slide down to Failure Valley
while recalling my triumph of Success Mountain
or...
Should I start the long and strenuous climb up to
the next peak of Success Mountain?

The choice is yours.

Some prefer the comfort of average flat ground.
While others will choose to coast for a while and
take the easy walk down the valley.

Few will persist
and do **Whatever It Takes**
to reach the next peak.

Those that continue up the next mountain
will soon realize that they already possess the
training, skills and stamina
to take on this next challenge.
Thanks to their momentum,
this one was more challenging
yet not quite as difficult
as the previous endeavor.

As for those that finally reach the valley floor
they can, unlike at the top,
stay down there for quite a while.
They may even come upon a lower valley that
they never even knew existed.

But when you finally decide to escape
the depths of the valley,
you will have a longer
and more strenuous journey ahead of you
that is only determined by
how far you previously descended down
upon the valley you now reside.

And now it will take even more effort than before,
just to get back to par (ground level.)

You will then have to decide again
if you wish to stay upon boring average ground
and catch your breath for a while
or...
take the easy walk back down to Failure Valley
or...
continue the long and strenuous climb up to the
next peak of Success Mountain.

Those people that are able to climb
from the deepest valleys to the highest peaks,
will encounter the longest journeys.

They will enjoy the same
temporary moments of success,
but will be even more humbled by the journey
and overwhelmed by their great success.

It is only from this grand new vista
that you will finally realize:

**There are deeper valleys to plunge into
and greater mountains to conquer**!

The choice is yours!

ASK BETTER QUESTIONS

**Believe it or not
you already possess
all the correct answers**

**The Key simply lies
in asking the right Questions**

What can I do today to improve my tomorrow?

What are the three most important things I need to accomplish today?

How can I improve the quality of my life?

What can I do today to improve my health?

How can I be a better wife, husband, friend, co-worker, etc?

What are my greatest assets?

What are my greatest weaknesses?

What skills do I need to further develop in order to become more successful?

What can I do differently or more efficiently?

How can I further simplify my life?

What am I most thankful for?

What have I already accomplished in my life?

What are my top three goals?

How can I live more creatively?

Is this _____ helping or hurting me?
Thought
Food
Drink
Drug
Decision
Indecision
Choice
Belief
Relationship

What type of people would I like to spend the most time and surround myself with?

Which modern day leaders or people do I admire and respect?

Who is living a lifestyle that I would like to live? What advice would these people give me to improve my current situation or challenge?

Ask better Questions
Search for better Answers
Expect
Exceptional
Outcomes

Never miss an opportunity

Always expect
chance encounters
open doors
and
open arms

IMPROVE YOUR FINANCES

We have all heard the expression, "Money is the root of all evil" but do not believe it. Money is not evil and I can prove it.

Have you ever donated money to a church or charity? Was that evil? What if you had more money to donate and gave more, would that be evil? What if you used your money to put a roof over your family, to feed them healthy foods and help them receive a higher education – would that be evil? Are there evil things that can be purchased with money? Absolutely! But there are far more things that can be purchased for good.

So from this point on remove all thoughts about your pursuit of money as being a sin and remember:

**It is the actions of the person
that determines the outcome
not the money itself**

What can I do today
to Improve my financial situation tomorrow?

It may seem conflicting to speak of money within a chapter entitled, "Satisfy Your Soul." But like it or not, we live in a Capitalistic World where everything has a price tag. Your food has a price tag, your home has a price tag, your dreams have a price tag. It is an unfortunate byproduct and reality of today's modern developed society.

So if money is a necessity for living in our modern World, then you might as well spend the eight hours a day at work doing something you enjoy – something you are Passionate about. For if you are not doing what you are put on this Earth to do **Right Now**, then how much longer will you wait to **Satisfy Your Soul**???

**To maximize my freedom
I must remain Cash Strong
and Debt Free**

ARE YOU SELF-EMPLOYED?

It is my belief that in the not too distant future, a majority of the population will be either self-employed or generating some sort of income from a side business.

Remove the labels of: job; employee; or independent contractor for just a moment, and realize that Your Life **IS** Your Business! Every dollar you earn and each dollar you spend reflects upon the bottom line of , "YOU Incorporated!" If you sell something on Craig's List, buy a new car or even save $5 on groceries this week – each financial transaction equates to a business decision.

We are each responsible for our own lives and financial futures, so work together with your spouse, your family, your friends or even start out on your own and figure out how to:

**Create
multiple streams
of residual income**

SECTION V

CONCLUSION

BRING IT ALL TOGETHER

"We are all the authors of our own lives.

Some of us write adventure,
some write romance,
yet others write tragedy.

Some of our books
are just more interesting than others.

If your book is boring you
then write a new chapter
and live what you want to read."

-from the book,
Happy, Healthy, Wealthy & Wise

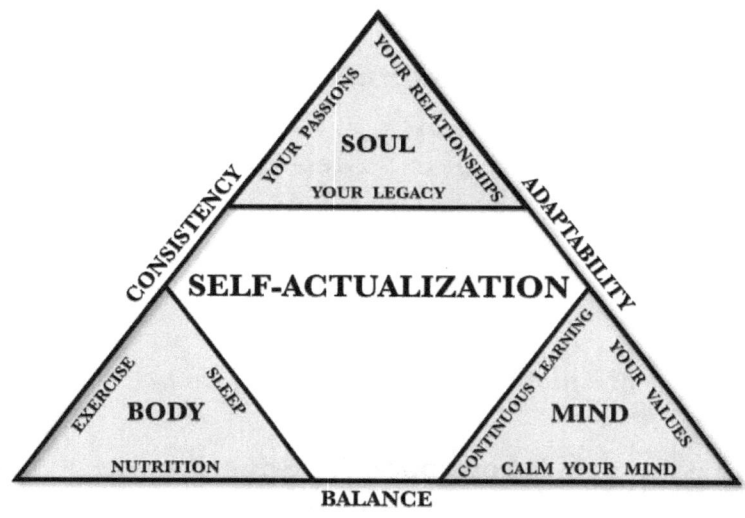

The Self-Actualization Pyramid
by: Eric J. Safranek

A CULMINATION
OF BOTH WORLDS

Follow these steps, one at a time sequentially, to ascend to a higher plane of not only existing, but truly living a meaningful life. There are no set goals prior to advancing to subsequent steps, but instead an ongoing marathon of achievements that are gradually improved upon lap after lap after lap. Each accomplishment enhances the next one, which in turn creates:

Infinite Loops of Perpetual Improvement.

First: **OPTIMIZE YOUR HEALTH**
Focus first upon Nutrition and the quality of fuel that you feed your Body. This first step lays the foundation, not only for your survival, but for success within all other steps. Then improve your body through Exercise and allow it the time it needs to recover through Sleep.

Second: **CULTIVATE YOUR MIND**
Focus first upon Calming Your Mind, for a scattered mind allows no room for higher levels of thought. Then continue your lifelong pursuit of Continuous Learning and fine-tuning your Values.

Third: **SATISFY YOUR SOUL**
Focus first upon discovering your Passions. Then work to pursue your Passions and improve your Relationships. As you realize your Passions and enhance the important Relationships in your life, so Your Legacy shall grow.

Fourth: **SELF-ACTUALIZE**
Bring it all together and discover your perfect Balance at each point in your life. Constantly Adapt and adjust to the changes within you, your life and the world all around you. The more Consistently you follow the steps of the Pyramid, the greater your results will be.

Lastly: **A CULMINATION OF BOTH WORLDS**
Understand that there is no end to your ongoing search for discovering your perfect Balance, Adapting to change, and the required Consistent practice of new habits. Life and all that thrives within it, are forever in a state of flux. Consistently aim to Adapt to and establish, a better Balance in each area of your life, for as you age: your goals, your priorities and your capabilities will change as well.

ROI

Which of my Actions
offer the greatest
Return On Investment?

Which offer the least?

Which _____ offer the best ROI?
Foods
Exercises
Expenditures
Sales Technique
Business Acquaintances

Properly answer these questions,
follow the results
and you shall discover
the path of least resistance
to your each and every goal

HOW TO BE HAPPY

Decide to be Happy

Allow yourself to be Happy

Constantly remind yourself to be Happy

Think Happy Thoughts and
read Inspirational Affirmations every day

Convincingly say it out loud...
"I AM HAPPY!"

Help a friend

Help a family member

Help a stranger

Laugh more

Smile

If seeking Happiness
look inward not outward
for your Happiness is formulated
within each and every decision

Happiness is always available to you

You carry it within you
wherever you go

The Key to Happiness
simply lies within your ability
to unlock the door
on a daily basis
and permit it to enter
your everyday life

Happy people are simply the ones
who ALLOW themselves to be Happy

Never allow the stress of today
the regrets of the past
or the anxiety of future
make you believe
for even one moment
that you do not deserve
the Happiness you seek

**Live today
within the moment
without regrets
for today
is another day
to get it right**

FINAL THOUGHTS

Let's say that you decide to accept all of my advice and choose to live your life around my teachings and in the end you lived an average life and didn't receive everything that you originally hoped for. Would you consider your life a failure?

Or, do you believe that living an Optimistic, Happy and Healthy Life with many close friends may be worth the gamble? Personally, I do not see the down-side in constantly attempting to Improve yourself as you Pursue Your Dreams.

**The greatest risk we face in life
is living a life
that wasn't worth living**

**A life without Passion
A life without Risk
A life without Love**

**Is not a Life
for me...**

A WORD OF CAUTION

There is such an abundance of information available to us nowadays. Much of which is purposefully deceiving and grossly inaccurate. From content marketing and random bloggers sharing their opinions, to corporate backed news organizations and TV channels that are dedicated to swaying elections and public opinion. You and You alone are responsible for filtering all this information, researching all these claims and deciding which of it applies to you and agrees with your personal morals and beliefs.

As you may eventually come to learn, the solutions do not lie to the extreme left or extreme right, but instead, somewhere in between.

Sports, Politics, Religion and controversial issues are but tactics utilized by both church and state in an attempt to divide and control citizens and constituents. You can defy this by seeking out common ground between yourself and others instead of continuing to promote these manipulative techniques.

IF EVERYONE FOLLOWS THEIR PASSION, WHO WILL DO ALL THE DIRTY WORK?

Here's a little secret...

Most people will not follow their Passions. Whether due to a limitless list of excuses, skepticism, lack of risk taking, lack of confidence, lack of drive and follow-through or simply from never taking the time to specifically define what it is that they want... most people will not follow their Passions.

So how can I become one of the few that actually follows my Passion?

Specifically define your Goals
Improve your Confidence
Eliminate Excuses
Take more Risks
and most importantly...
TAKE MORE ACTION!

If I were to summarize my overall philosophy and wrap it up in a nice little present for you, it would look something like this:

Become an Optimist

Constantly Improve Yourself

Eat more Nutritious Foods

Improve Your Health

Calm Your Mind

Increase Your Focus

Never stop Learning

Pursue Your Passions

Build strong Connections with many people

Create a Legacy that you can be proud of

Focus upon all the good things in your life
and do **WHATEVER IT TAKES**
to increase your personal Happiness
and the lives of the people all around you

So as I leave you now, I have three last questions for you:

Did you collect all the Keys?

**Which Keys or lessons
are most important to you?**

**Which Key do you believe is the Skeleton Key
that unlocks all the other doors?**

*"Shoot for the moon
and if you miss
you will still be among the stars."*

–Les Brown

I sincerely hope that you have enjoyed this book and the many lessons that it offers. It is my intention that each time you pick up this book, you will leave with at least one more insight that may improve upon the quality of your life and the world all around you!

I have included a Bonus Chapter at the end of this book for my readers entitled, "The AvanVive Way" which goes on to share my company's Philosophy, Strategy and Mission which we strive to achieve on a daily basis.

*May you live a
long and prosperous life!*

*A life full of Self-Improvement,
Simplicity and Compassion!*

An Optimistic and Creative Life!

*A life that is full of ENERGÍA and
Infinite Loops of Perpetual Happiness!*

*A Passionate Life that is
Happy, Healthy, Wealthy & Wise
and one that leaves a lasting Legacy
which inspires others
and lives on for eons!*

CHEERS!

~Eric

HELP ME, HELP YOU

In an attempt to Ask Better Questions, further Expand MY Thinking, and provide a wider array of insights to future books, I am asking for your help.   What Advice, Wisdom and Secrets to Living a Better Life can you share with us?

What is the best advice you have ever received?

*What steps have you taken
to improve the quality of your life?*

*"If you knew then, what you know now..."
What one thing in life would you do differently?*

What do you believe is your purpose on Earth?

*Years from now
when you are old and gray
what wisdom or advice would you pass on
to your 18 year old grandchild?*

Please share your answers with us at:

AvanVive@AvanVive.com

ASK AND YOU SHALL RECEIVE

If you enjoyed the book you just read, "***The Best of Both Worlds Theory***" I would greatly appreciate it if you could help us spread the word!

We are a start-up. Every single sale, piece of advice and Positive Review that we receive, makes all the difference in the World to us!

If you did enjoy the book, can you please go to:

Amazon.com

to, "Write a customer review" and award my book four or five stars. Please tell your friends, buy copies for your staff and connect with us on Facebook at:

www.Facebook.com/AvanVive

Thank you so much
for all your help and participation
in growing our
Small Business!

SECTION VI

BONUS CHAPTER!

THE AVANVIVE WAY

Live, Love, Work & Play...
The AvanVive Way!

WHAT IS AVANVIVE?

AVANVIVE, (pronounced: ahh-von-VEE-vay) comes from the French word, "**Avant-garde**" which means: *the advance group in any field whose works are characterized chiefly by unorthodox and experimental methods*; and the Italian word, "**Vivere**" which means: *to live; life; lifestyle.*

Simply defined, AvanVive means: *to live an advanced and unorthodox life!*

AvanVive is a Lifestyle Brand that promotes our, "**Live, Love, Work & Play... Anywhere in the World**" vision. We spread our message through books, merchandise and eco-friendly products to customers that share our Vision, Morals and Beliefs.

WHY AVANVIVE?

Nowadays, there is such an abundance of negativity out there. People focus upon pessimistic beliefs, pointless distractions and false ideologies. Many end up leading a meaningless life, lost and without direction. We believe that there is a better way to live life!

Here at AvanVive, we believe in **The Law of Attraction** and surrounding ourselves with others that are as Passionate about living a Positive life of constant Self-Improvement as we are. As a result, we attract more people of a similar mindset as well as everything we need in order to live a Successful and Purposeful life. We truly believe that The Path to a Successful life lies within discovering your Passions, increasing your Happiness and cultivating your Friendships. If you lead a Happy, Passionate life, surrounded by many friends and those you have helped, you will be blessed... in every sense of the word!

WHAT INSPIRED THIS BUSINESS?

Have you ever seen the movie, "The Matrix"? There is scene in the movie where Morpheus offers Neo the choice of a red pill or a blue pill. If Neo chooses the blue pill, the story ends. If he chooses the red pill, "you stay in Wonderland and I show you how deep the rabbit-hole goes."

The red pill for me was my experience working at Club Med. I worked off and on for about ten years at Club Med Resort Villages throughout the U.S., Caribbean and Mexico. It opened my eyes to a whole new way of living and looking at life. When I say that I worked with people from all over the world, I literally mean that I closely worked with, on average, 110 people from twenty-six different countries, for six months at a time! Now that is diversity!

They surrounded me with these beautiful people from all over the world and "forced" me to live in beautiful island villages and beach resorts! There were a plethora of languages spoken throughout the village and the idiosyncrasies were as diverse as the staff.

Now I'm not gonna pretend that we didn't have our differences, disagreements or communication breakdowns... we had plenty! BUT, for the most part, we all got along! It was almost like our own little model U.N. It was here at the Club Med Resorts that my eyes were first opened and I got to experience a better way to live my life.

First of all, I learned that I definitely preferred living on a beach in the Bahamas to shoveling snow in Chicago. Secondly, I loved meeting these people from all over the world and learning their unique perspectives. Third, we were truly living life to the fullest – we were, "Rock Stars without the instruments!" And lastly, these people were Happy! Our job was to be Happy and **Create Memorable Experiences** – not too shabby! We were having fun, enjoying life and we were making some of the best friends of our lives! It was no wonder why it was so easy for us to buy into their marketing campaigns:

"Club Med, The Antidote to Civilization"
and
"Club Med... Life as It Should Be"

WHAT IS THE MEANING
BEHIND OUR LOGO?

Our logo, which we refer to as, "**Globo de Pangaea**™" is a reference to the original orientation of our continents, one super-continent, referred to as Pangaea. We all share this commonality and though continental drift has separated us by oceans, we all come from the same soil and are simply pieces of a larger puzzle. We aim to bridge this gap by promoting our, **One World Philosophy** which we believe will unite us with our like-minded brothers and sisters in order to enjoy the one life we know we have, on the only planet that will tolerate us!

The seven continents represent our company's prime objectives:

Africa: **Philanthropy**

Antarctica: **Simplicity**

Asia: **Ethos**

Australia: **Environment**

Europe: **Wanderlust**

North America: **Business**

South America: **Health**

OUR VALUES

Planet Earth
We have but one planet and it is our primary objective to protect her by practicing and promoting Eco-friendly business practices and lifestyle improvements. We aim to connect with others and Create Meaningful Relationships with people from all over the globe as we work together towards larger goals and Improve our Planet.

Ethical Business Practices
Our goal is to run an ethical, (yet profitable) business while striving to work exclusively with other companies, corporations and small business owners that share this same benchmark.

Living a Happy, Healthy, Wealthy & Wise Life
Improving the Health, Education, Personal Finances, Happiness and overall well-being of our Employees and Customers alike.

Balance
We aim to improve the Work/Life Balance of our employees and customers as well as promote our Middle Way Philosophy.

Experiences
We believe in gathering Experiences instead of collecting possessions.

Philanthropy
Helping families and individuals all over the globe who are in need of financial support, educational tools and/or basic survival essentials.

Simplicity and Efficiency
We value living as simply as possible, alongside and in harmony with, the technology and advances of our modern day society, in an attempt to live as efficiently as possible.

Unity
We aim to Unify people instead of further dividing them. To present what we all have in common, instead of focusing upon what make us different.

Self-Improvement

We strive to improve ourselves and our company on a daily basis and never stop learning from our customers.

Diversity

It is our goal to promote equality in the work place, society, and all over the world, without regard to a person's sex, color, heritage, race, religion or sexual preference. We support Gay Rights and Gay Marriage. We support Women's Rights as well as their right to choose. We denounce the belittling and repression of any group of people due to any of the above characteristics. We do not believe in rushing to judgment or that a person is defined by a single action, word or phrase they may have said during a momentary lapse of judgment, but instead by the overall intent of their actions. At AvanVive, we celebrate and welcome diversity along with all of its challenges.

Worldwide Immigration Reform

We make efforts to reduce regulations and open up the boarders to World Travelers, Explorers and Adventurers from all over the Globe.

Cultural Cohesion

We encourage Learning new Languages and Exploring new Cultures in an attempt to communicate with, and better understand, our fellow humans.

That which makes Life worth living

Come together with others to Promote, Preserve and Enjoy all the Art, Music and Nature that crosses each continent and unites us all!

*"There is no passion
to be found playing small –
in settling for a life
that is less than the one
you are capable of living."*

-Nelson Mandela

THE AVANVIVE VISION

We at AvanVive have a Belief

**A Belief that if people are doing the work
they are Passionate about,
the World will become a better place**

**We believe that the more people we Motivate
to rediscover and pursue their Passions
the faster the World will improve**

**We believe that those who
follow their Passions
by leading a meaningful life
and fulfilling their purpose on this Earth
will become the leaders
who influence and create
the Positive Changes
all over the globe**

Live, Love, Work & Play...
Anywhere In The World! ™

THE AVANVIVE DREAM

Imagine a globe without borders

**Imagine discovering for yourself
all of the beauty and Adventure
that the World has to offer**

Imagine pursuing Love on any continent

**Imagine possessing the Freedom
to Live and Work
Anywhere in the World...**

This is the AvanVive Dream!

Traveling and living abroad has taught me so much and greatly contributed towards making me the person that I am today. One of the primary goals of this book is to promote International Travel amongst North Americans.

For it is my belief that the more people in the World who travel, the more similarities will be discovered, the more personal Connections will be made and the better we will become in improving Worldwide diplomacy.

Now I am not suggesting that you quit your job tomorrow and hit the road. What I am suggesting is that you live your life to the fullest and pursue your Passions, wherever on Earth they may guide you.

Start at home, explore your town and the cities that surround you, then expand out from there.

You cannot fully appreciate the overall experience and vastness of the Grand Canyon during the day or the romance of Paris at night simply from pictures alone. I highly suggest that you accumulate as many **Memorable Experiences** as you can collect over your lifetime! Go visit new countries, hold conversations with people that are different than you and try new things. For the lessons you learn from these experiences will never be fully replicated within the confines of a book or movie.

"Live, Love, Work & Play... Anywhere in the World" is not only the words we live by here at AvanVive, but also the title of one of my upcoming books! We are continually in the process of interviewing people from all over the world that are living an AvanVive kinda life!

If you Live, Love, Work and Play outside your country of citizenship or know of someone else who is, we would love to hear about it!

Please share your story with us at:

AvanVive@AvanVive.com

And remember, no matter your age, sex, ethnicity, background, citizenship or excuse, we all possess the potential and right to:

Live, Love, Work & Play...
  Anywhere in the World! ™

Also available from AvanVive Publishing:

...and remember to visit us at:

www.AvanVive.com

**To get the latest AvanVive Apparel
and Merchandise.**

ABOUT THE AUTHOR

Eric J. Safranek was born in the suburbs of Chicago in what was, at that time, the small city of Naperville, Illinois. A few years after graduating high school from Lake Zurich, Illinois, he become overwhelmed with wanderlust, hit the road and never looked back. These travels allowed him to not only backpack throughout Australia, but to also live and work throughout the US in: San Diego, California; Phoenix, Arizona; Copper Mountain, Colorado; Hilton Head Island, South Carolina; Savannah, Georgia; Fort Lauderdale, Florida; Orlando, Florida and St John, USVI. Thanks to working at Club Med Resort Villages off and on for over ten years, he was able to Live, Work and Play in: The Bahamas; Turks and Caicos; Dominican Republic as well as three different stints in Cancun, Mexico, including one final season in 2008 where he finally met his wife, Paula, who is from Venezuela. Eric and Paula currently reside in Florida as they continually pursue opportunities to...

Live, Love, Work & Play...
Anywhere in the World!